INTENTIONAL LOVE
31 Ways to Love Your husband WITH PURPOSE

LEAH HEFFNER

Copyright © 2017 by Matt and Leah Heffner

All rights reserved.

No part of this book may be reproduced or transmitted in any form or by any means, electronic or mechanical, including photocopying, recording, or by any information storage and retrieval system without the written permission of the author, except for the use of brief quotations in a book review.

Scripture quotations are from the ESV® Bible (The Holy Bible, English Standard Version®), copyright © 2001 by Crossway, a publishing ministry of Good News Publishers. Used by permission. All rights reserved.

To my husband Matt, our kids, the future generations, and the glory of God. — LH

TABLE of CONTENTS

Introduction 1
1: Love Story..10
2: I See You... 14
3: I Appreciate You...18
4: Patient..22
5: What You Look For.. 26
6: Notebook Doodles..30
7: I'm Sorry 34
8: Carve Out Time.. 38
9: Talk About Him 42
10: Cheerleader 46
11: Tech Free..50
12: Kind... 54
13: Hold Hands... 58
14: No Swooping.. 62
15: Self-Care... 66
16: Love Tank 70
17: 10-Second Kiss 74

18: Good Dad	78
19: Priority	82
20: Not Easily Angered	86
21: Question Game	90
22: Career	94
23: Go to Bed	98
24: Physical Attractiveness	102
25: Sex	106
26: Sleep	110
27: Do Something Together	114
28: Yes & No	118
29: Little Moments	122
30: Have Fun	126
31: Go Out	130
32+ Perseveres	134
Discussion Questions	140
Resource Page	145

INTRODUCTION

Hi there. We're so glad you've decided to join us for *Intentional Love*. We know it's no small thing to open a brand new book, willing to learn some new things. Especially when it comes to our marriages, which are no small things in and of themselves.

Intentional Love is 31 ways to love your husband with purpose. What *Intentional Love* was created to do is to give you encouragement to look at your marriage with intentionality, to make it a priority even in the fullest seasons of life, and to build the habits that will help you love your husband with purpose.

Each day should take you less than 10 minutes to read and complete the journal prompt. You can complete the Discussion Questions each day or in chunks as you go. The questions are found at the end of each day, in one list at the back of the book, and as a printable in the resources section. Some days, your topics will be the same as your husband's. And some days they will be different.

INTENTIONAL LOVE: 31 WAYS TO LOVE YOUR *husband*

This resource is intended for good intentioned marriages, or marriages that do not include the four A's: abuse, adultery, abandonment, or addiction. If any of the four A's are something you are working through in your marriage, we hope you will seek professional Christian help.

These habits are the same things that we use in our own marriage to make it a priority throughout the various and changing seasons that have and are occurring. These are the building blocks that we use to approach and connect with each other.

But these things alone are not enough for your marriage.

Even the best habits, the kindest actions, the most sincere and intentional moments alone can't fix, change, or support a marriage all on their own.

The motivation for these actions in our marriage has been and continues to be what Jesus did for us through His death on the cross and resurrection.

Without that basis, without marriage and the unity it creates reflecting the gospel, a marriage, even a marriage with the best of intentions, is just a shadow.

INTRODUCTION

But when our marriages are built on that truth, and we realize we need grace to grow into the husbands and wives God has in mind for us to be, we can start to see where being intentional in our marriages has such a huge impact.

We don't always get it right. We don't have a magic formula for marriages. We know that showing up, again and again, is worth it. Marriage is a sanctifying process that is worth the mistakes, trying again, and growing by grace.

Marriage is about showing up, day after day, and committing to learn and relearn things about your husband and how you can intentionally love him. When you got married, whether it's been a couple of years or a couple of decades ago, you promised to love a moving target, someone who would grow and change over the years. And this promise to love is a promise to choose to love, to show love, and to choose them again and again.

You could go through this book with your husband over the course of the next month or you can feel free to take longer to give more attention to the days that need a little extra TLC. This book isn't the boss of you, so feel free to go through it at your own pace. (There are times when we reference the "month" but if you don't do it that way, no problem!)

INTENTIONAL LOVE: 31 WAYS TO LOVE YOUR *husband*

You could nail every topic, every discussion question thrown your way. Or you could struggle to make your actions line up with your head and your heart.

All of this is normal and is a part of the journey of marriage. We don't think this will end for you in 31 days, even if you've finished each of the activities. It certainly hasn't ended for us.

You may find yourself really impacted by a few of these days and choose to continue to focus on them after this month is finished.

You may find yourself circling back around to specific days in certain situations or to the entire book as you enter other seasons.

We pray that this book is a resource that encourages and emboldens you to make your marriage a priority, right in the middle of whatever you have going on in your life. To choose to love your husband intentionally, and with purpose.

In light of all of this, and in light of the heart work that you're setting out to do, we would like to encourage you to assume good will from your husband. There may be days when he doesn't complete the activity in the way or the time frame you hoped he would. That's ok.

INTRODUCTION

We encourage you to let go of your expectations for him and any activities associated with this book and instead focus on yourself, your heart, and what you're doing and learning throughout this book. We know this isn't easy, but we also know that you only have control over your own actions, and how you choose to serve and love. How your husband goes through and processes this information may not look the same as the way you would go through and process this information.

The action changes and heart work that we pray will take place beginning over the next month are not about measuring each other or measuring up. It's about choosing to show up, love up, and look up to the One who created marriage and wants to see us invested in it.

Before we kick off these 31 days together, we'd like to take some time to pray for our hearts and our marriages. Real change is heart-level stuff and the heart work you're about to start will impact you in lots of different ways.

INTENTIONAL LOVE: 31 WAYS TO LOVE YOUR *husband*

So, today and every day of this challenge let's pray for our marriages.

Be praying that your heart would have pure motives for these changes.

Be praying that your actions would help to change your thoughts and your feelings.

Be praying that you would react well to what your husband tries over the next month.

Be praying that you would put your attention and effort into each day's lesson.

Be praying that the two of you would come together more during this time.

Be praying that you would learn much during this time.

Be praying that the effects would spill over into all areas of your life.

Be praying that you would have grace with yourself for the activities that are challenging.

Be praying that you would extend grace to your husband for the activities that don't go so well.

INTRODUCTION

If it feels overwhelming to pray through this list, we've written out a short prayer on the next page that you can pray through right now and each day before you begin.

We are so excited that you've decided to work on your marriage by choosing intentional love.

Keep up with us over the course of the month with the hashtag #intentionallove31.

— Matt and Leah

P.S. If you have little kids at home, you'll need to plan a babysitter for Day #31. Trust us on this one.

INTENTIONAL LOVE: 31 WAYS TO LOVE YOUR *husband*

Dear Lord,

I pray that you would do a work in my heart over the next month. As I work through different actions to love my husband well each day, I ask that you would give me a humility that I haven't known before. Humility to understand clearly what you might teach me and how you might change my heart during this time.

I pray, Lord, that you would help me to be willing and excited each day to love my husband. Regardless of how he reacts or what he might do for me. Help me to pursue his heart with abandon. I know that I want to see results right away but that's not often how you work, Lord. Help me to have patience and joy during this next month.

As I feel my way through some new things I know that it might be messy. I pray that you would help me to love well. To give my husband so much grace. And, to give myself so much grace. Thank you Lord for the opportunity to be married and grow closer with my husband.

In Jesus' Name Amen.

INTRODUCTION
THINK AND JOURNAL

INTENTIONAL LOVE

1

love story

1: LOVE STORY

Every love story is beautiful, but ours is my favorite.
— Anonymous

The story of how my husband and I met, started dating, and eventually fell in love and got married has some funny parts, especially at the beginning.

Like, I couldn't remember who he was the first time I met him but he thought I was joking.

He thinks I tricked him into going on a double date before he was ready (but it wasn't a date because I don't usually talk about the profit margins of ice cream joints on dates).

We cannot agree on what or when our first date actually was.

I knew he had the ring to propose but I thought he'd wait another six months or so to pop the question. So when someone asked me when we'd get engaged, I snort-laughed and said "never!"
He proposed that night.

And while there were blunders and missteps, our love story is definitely my favorite (no offense to yours, which I'd also love to hear sometime.)

Your love story doesn't have to be Hollywood magic (mine definitely isn't). It doesn't have to look like anyone else's. It doesn't have to be anything specific.

INTENTIONAL LOVE: 31 WAYS TO LOVE YOUR *husband*

The fact that it's *yours* is what makes it special. The fact that you can see how God worked and orchestrated behind the scenes to have you meet at the right time and that He brought your hearts together.

Love stories are beautiful things. We love watching them, listening to other people's, and even telling our own.

We are building our own love stories every day. Not every day will be perfect, but when we work through the hard days and seasons, we will be able to look back and see how we've grown, how we've been blessed, and how far we've come.

Think and Journal

Think about your love story and some of the major milestones. Write them down. Then think about how you'd like to share that story with your kids one day. Will it be in a story? Will it be in pieces over time? Will it be in one big epic chunk when you're old and gray?

Intentional Love

Share some of your favorite milestone memories with your husband. You can write it out on a sticky note or in something a little longer if you'd like. You can simply share a memory or reminisce for hours. And ask for some of his.

Discussion Question

Talk about what you'd like your love story legacy to be and how you want to share that with your kids or other people around you.

1: LOVE STORY

THINK AND JOURNAL

INTENTIONAL LOVE

2

i see you

2: I SEE YOU

My husband and I often say that if it weren't for our kids, we'd be workaholics. It is really easy for us to focus in on a task, an achievement, and work at it until we complete it, achieve the thing, open the door, and move onto the next task.

I know this because we spent the first year of our marriage, in our apartment, in separate rooms, working late into the evening, using our focus and attention on work instead of on each other. I'm certainly not saying we spent no time on our marriage, I'm just being honest about our focus.

And so I know how easy it is to get distracted from each other, and the more life we have going on and swirling around us, the more easily distracted we can be.

What you look for is what you see. So you can focus on the other things going on around you or you can work on learning how to focus on each other.

In this stage of life, one of the most life-giving phrases I keep in mind is "I see you". And then, I work to see my husband more.

I look to see what he's doing and what he's done to serve us.

I listen to what he's thinking and planning; what he's excited and worried about.

I notice what he's interested in and learning about.

INTENTIONAL LOVE: 31 WAYS TO LOVE YOUR *husband*

"I see you" are some deeply powerful words and we can use them so well in our marriages by choosing to focus on the good things about our husbands.

Think and Journal

Make a list of things you've noticed your husband do this week, things you've heard him talk about whether that's work or other interests. Write as many things as you can think of.

Intentional Love

Continue to notice things that your husband does to serve and love your family.

Discussion Questions

Ask: What types of things do you wish I'd notice more? When do you feel the most seen: When you are thanked/acknowledged? When you are given a break from those things? When you are helped with those things? When you're given affirmations for those things?

2: I SEE YOU

THINK AND JOURNAL

INTENTIONAL LOVE

3

i appreciate you

3: I APPRECIATE YOU

Often, we'll hear "motherhood is a thankless job".

And to be honest, so is marriage.

But it doesn't have to be.

We promised to choose to love a moving target for the rest of our lives on this earth, and that is no small thing!

And then there are about a million small, medium, and big things that go into our everyday lives together, from taking out the trash, to figuring out the budget, to finding a house, to grocery shopping. And the list literally goes on and on and on.

The life we're building together isn't just the big things — it's all the things. And the things that hold us together the most are often the smallest things.

We've taken the time to say "I see you" and today we're going to take the time to say "I appreciate you".

I appreciate you for going to work. For working with me on that hard topic. For letting me take a nap when you really needed one too. For choosing me again today.

INTENTIONAL LOVE: 31 WAYS TO LOVE YOUR *husband*

Think and Journal

Make a list of big, medium, and small things you appreciate and are thankful for in your husband. Set a timer. And see how many you can get listed in five minutes.

Intentional Love

Write the things from the list in a note. That way it's something he can keep and look at and remember what you appreciate about him.

Discussion Question

Ask: How do you like to be thanked? With a note, gesture, in the moment, later, in front of people, or privately? Talk about your preferences.

3: I APPRECIATE YOU

THINK AND JOURNAL

INTENTIONAL LOVE

4

patient

4: PATIENT

I am not by nature a super patient person.

I buy birthday gifts for other people and I want to give them as soon as I get them home. Nothing ever cooks or bakes fast enough, so I tend to turn up the heat and rush it. When I decide there's something on the shopping list I need, Amazon Prime is rarely fast enough to get it to me.

But my husband, he is patient.

He takes things as they come. Lingers over meals. Explains things to our kids at length.

And our timelines of how we see things moving have always been just slightly off, as I speed through and he savors through.

This difference reminds me that love is patient. It's patient with timelines, with growth, with waiting, and with the other person who is different than you are.

We can't zoom through to being married 50, 60 or even 80 years. We have to take it as it comes, the ups and downs, the goods and bads, the betters and worses, and the richers and poorers.

This is growing together without the deep sighs, and the annoyances, and the anxiously waiting for the next stage. But intentionally choosing to show up, even in this stage, and to be patient through it.

Because love is patient.

Think and Journal

Which of the two of you is more patient? Do you feel like your speeds are really different or pretty similar? Have they become more so or less so over the course of your marriage? How would you like to grow in patience?

Intentional Love

Be patient with your husband today in a way that works out your patience muscle. Maybe that's waiting for him to share more about his day or waiting to speak to him until he has his eyes on you.

Discussion Question

Ask: In what ways do you feel like I'm most/least patient with you?

4: PATIENT

THINK AND JOURNAL

INTENTIONAL LOVE

5

what you look for

5: WHAT YOU LOOK FOR

When we were in a particularly hard season, I jumped right on the complaining train and I had no intention of getting off. I spent most of the time I got to talk to my husband pointing out hard or perceived hard things about my day.

All I could see was the hard things all around me.

Until one day, my husband encouraged me to think of things that were good about my day, things I could be thankful for.

I didn't know exactly where to start. I had grown so accustomed to complaining that it felt hard.

At first, I begrudgingly made this change. I would think of something about our kids quickly so I could get back to complaining. I'd offer the one good thing as an afterthought.

My husband encouraged me again to work from that one thing to another and then another.

Then I realized that the more and more things I thought of that were good about my day, the easier it was to think of things that were good about my day.

Slowly, my complaining and grumbling changed to good things I saw throughout my days. Even good things I was learning to see in challenging situations.

What I look for is definitely what I see.

INTENTIONAL LOVE: 31 WAYS TO LOVE YOUR *husband*

And that's true with my husband, too.

I can focus on his flaws or shortcomings, which are there because we all have them, or I can choose to see the amazing things about him, and there are TONS.

If one of those things is going to grow, I'd love to see more of the good things grow.

Think and Journal

Make a list of things that you think are great about your husband. His character, how he cares for your family, specific things about him as a husband and father. Adjectives that describe him.

Intentional Love

Sit down with a blank piece of paper in front of you. Write your husband's name on the paper, right in the middle. Set a timer for five minutes. And write all the great things about your husband on your piece of paper that you can in that time. When the timer dings, stop. Save this and give it to him when you get to your discussion questions this week or for Day 31. (P.S. This is a great one to keep to read over and over!)

Discussion Question

We all know there are challenging things we will still see in our marriages and in each other. Ask: How would you like me to approach topics when change might be necessary or important?

5: WHAT YOU LOOK FOR

THINK AND JOURNAL

INTENTIONAL LOVE

6

notebook doodles

6: NOTEBOOK DOODLES

I have a confession to make — I was SO the girl in middle school who doodled and scribbled hearts all over her notebooks, played MASH without ceasing, and imagined who I might one day marry as I practiced my signature. Mrs. J.T.T. for the win.

And in many ways, I've grown and matured over the years. And in some ways I have not.

Like how I still love telling the world I'm crushing on my husband.

And I'm not so sure that's a bad thing.

When I create a password on my phone or computer, something I am going to have to input day after day, I try to choose something that will make me think of my husband. His name, our anniversary, or my personal fave "IloveMatt". I full on embrace my inner middle school girl.

Here's why I love this little trick — sometimes I will sit down at my laptop, still huffing and puffing and internal dialoguing about something that just happened. Then, I have to log into my computer and I have to type ilovematt. Which is a small thing. But it makes me stop and think.

Oh, of course, I do love him.

And that helps take the edge off, helps me focus on good things, and get over small things.

INTENTIONAL LOVE: 31 WAYS TO LOVE YOUR *husband*

If I had known my husband in middle school, I probably would have tried a couple of Mrs. Leah Heffner signatures on my notebook.

But my computer password is a pretty great grown up option.

Think and Journal

What are little ways you remind yourself of your husband throughout your busy day? If you aren't doing any, what are a few things you might like to start?

Intentional Love

Change a password, access code, or something else to a word, phrase, or number that reminds you of your husband. Choose something highly used, like your phone pass screen or your tablet login.

Discussion Question

Ask: What is something you do every day that makes you think of me?

6: NOTEBOOK DOODLES

THINK AND JOURNAL

INTENTIONAL LOVE

7

i'm sorry

7: I'M SORRY

"I'm sorry" is a powerful phrase that packs a big punch. Some people offer apologies freely, wanting to quickly mend the problem or perceived problem. And some people offer them rarely or not at all, letting the situation and actions speak for themselves. And there's a ton of shades of grey anywhere in between.

I'm an "I'm sorry" sayer. Problem? "I'm sorry." Perceived problem? "I'm sorry." I came to you with something I needed to tell you about that you did or said and you reminded me of my part in it? "I'm sorry."

Early in our relationship, my husband asked me if I just said sorry to try to make things better, to fix it, and move on without really having to change. And you know, I probably did that a lot. I thought an "I'm sorry" would just make the majority of the problems go away.

But "I'm sorry" isn't worth a lot if it's not backed up by change. Saying "I'm sorry" is a part, but actually changing the actions, thought processes, and the landscape for how the same situation goes down the next time is another.

A complete apology offers two parts — remorse, knowing and feeling that what you did was wrong, and repentance, turning from the wrong action and by grace, changing it.

So, yes, say sorry when you're wrong. It's important to learn to offer an apology when you make a mistake and know it. That's the remorse.

But then also back it up with actions and changes that show that you mean the sorry. That's the repentance.

INTENTIONAL LOVE: 31 WAYS TO LOVE YOUR *husband*

Think and Journal

What kind of sorry-sayer are you? A "say it and get it over with"? A "say it too much"? A "say it not enough or not at all?" Why do you think that is?

Intentional Love

We all make mistakes. Think of something that has caused a problem in the last week and really apologize for it using a five-point apology: 1. I'm sorry. 2. Here's what I did wrong. 3. Please forgive me. 4. I'll try not to do it again/I see this is something I can work on. 5. How can I make it up to you/Here's how I plan on making it up to you.

Discussion Question

Ask: Why do you think you are the kind of sorry-sayer you are? Was it modeled for you? Did you have to become a peacemaker in some way? Did you not see people apologize?

7: I'M SORRY

THINK AND JOURNAL

8: CARVE OUT TIME

Years ago, I came home from a MOPS meeting with what I thought was both a strange idea and brilliant concept. A weekly at home date night. Once a week. After the kids are in bed.

It was strange because even at that point, with one kid and one on the way, I couldn't imagine needing to schedule that kind of time. Wouldn't we just WANT to spend time together?

And it also seemed brilliant because it seemed like something that would be so simple to implement. No big hurdles to jump to make it happen. Just a date night.

When I mentioned it to my husband, it was met with a slight resistance, no doubt for some of the same reasons I resisted it.

But we did it.

We put a weekly date night on the calendar.

We take turns planning the night's activities. We don't answer our phones or work. We spend time together.

We've played board games, gotten take out for dinner, cooked a fancier meal after the kids are in bed, watched shows together. We've taken couples massage classes online and written out our bucket lists together.

INTENTIONAL LOVE: 31 WAYS TO LOVE YOUR *husband*

This weekly carved out time has become pretty sacred to us. We say no to other things to protect this time together and it's always great to reconnect after a crazy week.

Think and Journal

What would you like to see in your intentional, carved out time? Daily? Weekly? Certain activities? Certain relaxation or wind down things? If you want to do a bigger activity or a date night, search on Pinterest, and get ideas ready. That way, when you talk about carving out the time you'll know what kind of things you might want to do.

Intentional Love

Look at your calendar and choose a night every week that can be intentional, carved out time. This should be a night that's consistently free of meetings and other obligations or can be made consistently free of anything else. Put it on your calendar and start having intentional time this week.

Discussion Question

Discuss your ideal intentional, carved out time at home. Is there a meal? A theme? A pattern? Or would you want it to be different all the time?

8: CARVE OUT TIME

THINK AND JOURNAL

9: TALK ABOUT HIM

In a group of women, there are two kinds of stories that often dominate the landscape. One is childbirth stories — can't miss the chance to one-up the lady who was in labor for three hours with a five-pounder — and husband blunders.

This has taken a turn in my lifetime as I've watched TV dads become blundering idiots who couldn't hope to make it on their own if their wives didn't sweep in and save them from themselves and their own idiocy, rinse, and repeat.

But just because that's what's "normal" doesn't mean we have to participate.

On the contrary, being in a group of other people is a great opportunity to build up your husband.

I'm not saying make all the other ladies feel bad about their husbands. But if they can only point out bad things about their husbands, make a mental checklist of things you're thankful for. Say out loud something he did that you found specifically helpful in the last week.

What we look for is what we see. And when we spend our time looking for flaws we will see more flaws.

This one is an easy slippery slope, at least for me. I want to relate! Share my story! Say "I get ya sister!" but afterward, I feel yucky. Like I just ate poison. Because it was more important to me in that moment that I have something to say instead of paying attention to what I was doing.

You can be the different lady in the group. The one who is quiet about her husband or notices his great qualities. And that can start today.

Think and Journal

There are certain people who make it easier for us to be loose-lipped. Make a mental or written list of those people. Be aware of who they are so that you can mentally and prayerfully prepare to be around them. Write a prayer to protect your lips when you're with others.

Intentional Love

This week (today if you can!) say something great about your husband to a group of other people.

Discussion Question

Ask: How do you feel when you overhear me talking negatively about you in a group? How do you feel when you overhear me talking positively about you in a group?

9: TALK ABOUT HIM

THINK AND JOURNAL

10: CHEERLEADER

When I first met my husband, his plans for after school were exciting, but very different than what I had imagined.

He wanted to start his own business (yay!) flipping houses (cool!) and since he didn't have a lot of capital, he wanted to live in them as he did the work (wait what?).

I expressed my concerns. "So do you envision a lot of power tools laying around if we have small children?" "Will I have to jump over holes in the floor to go to the bathroom?" "You're cool with take out for dinner most nights, right?"

But I also set my mind to being on his team for this. We'd look for hours at real estate websites, combing through options and imagining and dreaming.

He never started a real estate flipping business. But since we graduated he has started his own business which has changed some over the years and we've talked through easily another 50 ideas.

Your husband may not have the entrepreneurial itch, but he definitely has dreams, things he'd like to try.

Be on his team. Don't point out the flaws of the plan or ways he'd need to grow first. Be encouraging. Be supportive. You can go through the pro and con list later.

First show up, with your pom poms, and be his cheerleader. He can do this! Let's figure out how!

INTENTIONAL LOVE: 31 WAYS TO LOVE YOUR *husband*

Think and Journal

When you and your husband plan and dream about the future, how do the conversations usually go? Do you feel heard? Does he? Take a few minutes and write a script of what the conversation usually looks like. And then take a few minutes and write a script for what you'd like it to look like the next time.

Intentional Love

Sit down together and look each other in the eye. Ask about something new he would like to try. Listen intently to his answer. It could be big — like a business, or small — like paddleboarding. Ask questions that dig deeper like "Tell me more about that" and "Where did you first hear about this" or "What really interests you about this". Don't point out flaws with the idea. Just listen. Encourage with your words and your expression.

Discussion Question

Ask: How do you normally feel in a conversation about your dreams? How would you like me to respond?

10: CHEERLEADER

THINK AND JOURNAL

11: TECH FREE

We all know our dependence on technology is no small thing. Most days my kids ask me a question that I have NO idea of the answer to and they say "Mom, just ask Google."

Our phones, computers, tablets, and TVs are our constant companions for entertainment, work, shopping, games, and more.

Often, we women think we are the masters of multitasking but if we want to really do something well, we know we can really only do one thing well at a time.

And I know I can't pay attention as well when I'm trying to be in more than one place — whether in my thoughts or actions.

We're dying for connection with real and beautiful things. We want real, oxytocin (the cuddle and connection hormone) connection from building a lasting relationship together. We want the dopamine (the do it again hormone) drip that makes us want to do it again and again.

And we're settling for the less-than dopamine drip of scrolling and distraction from our real life. We're settling for perceived relationship building by "liking" an acquaintance's social media post.

Work, TV, Instagram, and my newsfeed can all wait. My husband shouldn't have to.

INTENTIONAL LOVE: 31 WAYS TO LOVE YOUR *husband*

There are lots of ideas for combatting this. A few are: a tech basket for devices when it's family time. Designated no phone times. Asking the other person if they mind you using your phone when you're with them for a specific task then putting it right back away again.

Think and Journal

At what time of day does the allure of your devices start to suck you in? Brainstorm some ideas to cut down the allure. Maybe turn it off or set app timers. Try listening to a podcast or soundtrack so you're less likely to scroll.

Intentional Love

Start a habit today of choosing one less way to be susceptible to your technology. If you need ideas, you can see the resources in the back of the book.

Discussion Question

Ask your husband when your tech time bothers him the most. Listen to his ideas and work to not let technology continue to be a distraction from your marriage.

11: TECH FREE

THINK AND JOURNAL

INTENTIONAL LOVE

12

kind

12: KIND

Many of us have heard the expression "If you don't have anything nice to say, don't say anything at all."

And we teach this to our kids and we're taught it as children, but as we get older I feel like we use it less and less.

And we tend to use it less with those who are closest to us.

It's really easy when you're up close with someone, day in and day out, seeing all their stuff, the good stuff and bad stuff, to take notice of the not so great stuff about them.

And then to share that freely with them, often in criticism, or perceived criticism, nagging, or nit picking.

The reality is we all have flaws, things we could work on, should work on, need to work on.

I know my husband has flaws. I also have lots of my own.

I know it's my job to help him become the best version of himself, but I'm not his Holy Spirit, and focusing only on areas he needs to improve won't help him grow. It might even make him retreat, feeling like he can never get anything right.

What you look for is what you see. And you can cultivate kindness by choosing to look for good things and building goodwill in your marriage by speaking kindness into your husband.

INTENTIONAL LOVE: 31 WAYS TO LOVE YOUR *husband*

In our marriage, after building this habit over time, this has given me the ability to notice and speak to him about something that needs to be addressed — with kindness, respect, and humility. It can take the time to build this habit. But it's definitely one worth building.

Think and Journal

Are there certain events or scenarios when it feels easier to nit pick or be unkind? For me I've noticed there are certain triggers to me being unkind — usually lacking in sleep or spending extended time away from home. What are some of yours?

Intentional Love

Starting today, before you respond to anything, take a deep breath and remember that you can choose to be quiet if you can't figure out how to be kind. If the situation is an easy one, proceed as normal. If it's a tense situation, use the time to decide, what, if anything you want to say in the increased emotional state. Keep practicing this (it takes LOTS of time, but you have a lifetime).

Discussion Question

Ask: If there is an issue I would like to talk with you about, how can I handle it in a way that makes you feel loved and cared for?

12: KIND

THINK AND JOURNAL

INTENTIONAL LOVE

13

hold hands

13: HOLD HANDS

Did you know that otters hold hands while they're sleeping at night to keep from drifting away from one another?

I love otters. They are cute, playful, full of energy, and they remind me of something important.

We have a choice — we can grab a hold of our husband's hand and stay together with intentionality, even in the darkest nights. Or we can drift apart.

One of us has to be the first one to reach out a hand — to reach out for and hold onto the hand of the otter, er, other person.

I don't know about you, but I used to hold my husband's hand all the time. While we were driving. Sitting at the table. On the couch. As we fell asleep at night. At church. While we walked.

Lots of hand holding.

Now that we're outnumbered, we don't tend to have as many hands free to hold each other's. But we also don't seize as many opportunities as we do have.

I want to be more like an otter, reaching out to hold his hand when I feel like we could be drifting apart, when the days are tense and emotions are running high.

I want to reach out a hand as we drift off to sleep so we can be sure to drift together.

Think and Journal

Make a short list of the times when you are free to hold hands, even if it might be for just a few seconds.

Intentional Love

Hold hands tonight while you fall asleep. Look for opportunities to hold hands more often throughout the day. They are there!

Discussion Question

Ask: What are some of your favorite ways to connect through touch? How can we increase these occurrences during our busy days?

13: HOLD HANDS

THINK AND JOURNAL

INTENTIONAL LOVE

14

no swooping

14: NO SWOOPING

There is a lot that can be done in the name of help. And of course, I absolutely want to help my husband. And as a bonus, my husband's love language is acts of service, so help is kind of like love juice around my house.

But swooping is not helping.

In fact, swooping does a lot more hurting.

Wondering what swooping is? Swooping is, because you are able and capable and strong, you see something that your husband said he would do and hasn't gotten to yet, and you think "Well I can do that thing" and SWOOP and you do it for him in the name of helping.

I did this when we brought home our toddler bed to transition one kid from a crib. The neighbors gave us the bed and I brought it in the house as my husband left for work. He said he'd put it together for me. I was pregnant and he wanted to do it (in hindsight, for probably a lot of really good reasons).

But, I convinced myself that he worked long hours, and he didn't need something else on his plate, and besides I was plenty capable and SWOOP.

I had that bed together before he got home that night.

And as I proudly showed him the work I had done, the look on his face wasn't excitement. It was crushed. I had swooped and taken from him a chance to serve me, in the middle of me being pregnant and him working long hours and showing me love in the way that makes the most sense to him.

As a recovering swooper, I feel like I should let you know that this means things don't happen on my timeline. Things sometimes get forgotten. Sometimes these forgotten or missed things cost us some money or time we weren't planning on outputting.

But I'm meant to be my husband's helper — that means helping him be the best version of himself according to God's will. And if I swoop in on my timeline, he won't have a chance to grow.

I want to help my husband grow.

Think and Journal

Are you a Swooper? Close cousins of a Swooper are a Nagger, a Badger, and a Steamroller. Can you think of a specific time you swooped, nagged, badgered, or steamrolled? Write it down.

Intentional Love

Apologize for the incident you journaled about. Use the five-step apology from *I'm Sorry*.

Discussion Question

Ask: What's a way I swoop in, nag, badger, or steamroll you in something you say you'll take care of? How can I support you better?

14: NO SWOOPING

THINK AND JOURNAL

INTENTIONAL LOVE

15

self-care

15: SELF-CARE

I don't think I really "got" self-care for a long time. "Me time" felt selfish because it seemed like me vs them, my husband and kids.

But what I didn't realize was that I kind of was doing self-care all along, without even realizing it. By working, writing, and choosing to attend a Bible study, I was taking care to be built into, and I didn't even know I was doing it.

Self-care is the intentional way we pour and build into ourselves so that we can pour and build into the people around us in better ways.

Maybe this is something that's not even on your radar. Maybe you're in survival mode and you haven't even given this a thought.

Maybe you've thought about it but can't seem to make it work anywhere in the schedule. There's just nothing and nowhere to give with little kids and work and marriage and people that want to eat every day.

And maybe you're ready to clear a path to make some self-care happen because you know just how important it is.

Realize that whatever season you're in with needing self-care, that your husband is probably right there, too. We (us and our husbands) are, after all, one, and we go through our lives together. If you're in a tired, survival season, he probably has extra on his plate making him feel a similar way.

You BOTH need self-care time so you can build into your marriage.

INTENTIONAL LOVE: 31 WAYS TO LOVE YOUR husband

Think and Journal

Make a list of things you would like to do take care of yourself. Something creative? Physical? Social? Think about how much time and cost is involved with each one.

Intentional Love

Check your calendar for an hour or more of free space and suggest your husband use some of it for self-care and you use some as well!

Discussion Question

Sit down and talk about carving time out for both of you to get some self-care time. Maybe that's trading a couple hours every other Saturday. Maybe it's after the kids are in bed one night a week. Maybe it's on your lunch hour from work. Put it on the calendar.

15: SELF-CARE

THINK AND JOURNAL

16: LOVE TANK

Do you know what your love language is? What about your husband's?

I think we often assume we know what it is and that leads us to miss the mark, even if it's ever so slightly.

Like my top 3 are actually pretty close — physical touch, quality time, and acts of service. And that acts of service one just grows and grows the longer I'm a mom.

But for the longest time, we could not figure out my husband's.

Sure, I THOUGHT I knew it. I would pinpoint what I was SURE it was and then do all of these things for him.

Like when I thought it was words of affirmation, and I wrote him 31 days of letters and prayers and he said "thank you", set it on his desk for a few months, and then later confessed that it wasn't the Ah-ha, feeling super loved moment that either of us had hoped for.

So eventually, we cracked and took the assessment and found out his was acts of service.

I think one thing that the 5 *Love Languages* book misses is that we all have a way we give love best and a way we receive love best. For some people, that's the same. My husband gives and receives in acts of service.

INTENTIONAL LOVE: 31 WAYS TO LOVE YOUR husband

But I receive in quality time, physical touch, and acts of service, but I give in acts of service.

Knowing this has made some things a lot easier and more obvious. Like I know the best way to make him feel loved is to make sure he has clean underwear and undershirts for work.

But it's also helped me to be able to understand that he is definitely showing me that he loves me, even if it's not my first love language.

Think and Journal

Do you know your love language? Or think you know it? What about how you give vs. how you receive love?

Intentional Love

Take your 5 Love Languages Assessment out loud together, if you can (link in the resources). That way you hear each other's answers and preferences and can tuck them away for later.

Discussion Question

Share how you give and receive love, especially if they're different. Ask: What are 5 ways I could make you feel the most loved?

16: LOVE TANK

THINK AND JOURNAL

INTENTIONAL LOVE

17

10-second kiss

17: 10-SECOND KISS

Remember back when you first started kissing your husband and you like, never wanted to stop kissing?

I think about a week into kissing my husband, I seriously considered buying stock in the Chapstick company. My lips were parched, but I just didn't want to stop kissing him.

Somewhere along the way, we start kissing less.

Or we worry that kissing might "start something" or that he'll want more than a kiss.

We've got to bring back the kissing.

Give him a 10-second kiss before he walks out the door in the morning and when he comes back at night. Stop him when you pass him in the hallway. Pull him close while you make dinner. And then again while you clean up dinner. Lay one on him before he drifts off to sleep at night.

And maybe you will "start something" (besides a habit that will make the world stop for just the two of you, just for a moment) but is that really the WORST thing that could happen? Then it's still pretty stinkin' good.

INTENTIONAL LOVE: 31 WAYS TO LOVE YOUR *husband*

Think and Journal

Make a list of five times during a normal day when you could stop for a 10-second kiss.

Intentional Love

Start today! Give him a 10-second kiss whenever you see the chance.

Discussion Question

Ask: What is something specific you enjoy when I kiss you?

17: 10-SECOND KISS

THINK AND JOURNAL

18: GOOD DAD

Shortly after my husband and I started dating, I met his whole family. He's the oldest of five, definitely the treasured oldest brother, and has always been very involved with his siblings.

When I saw him interact with his brothers and sisters, I started swooning even harder, as I realized what kind of dad he would be.

And now, almost a decade later, I get the joy of watching him be a dad every single day.

He doesn't do everything the way I would do it. He has strengths and soft spots and all kinds of things that make us complement one another in our parenting and also reminds us of our differences.

He wrestles when I would rather sit and read. He tickles at bedtime when I'm inclined to tuck in and scoot. He takes time to imagine and dream when I'm more likely to tell the kids that no, you can't just ride a hot air balloon whenever you want.

He is such a good dad.

And the best way I know to keep him growing as a good dad is to point out the ways he already is a good dad so that he can continue to grow in those ways and then in new ways.

It can be really easy, especially in what feels like the never-ending high-stakes of parenting, to feel like we need to point out all the ways that the other person can improve.

Instead, let's choose to believe that what we look for is what we see — and we can choose to see the ways he is a good dad.

(Hey, we aren't parents! What should we do? Start noticing things about him that will make him a great dad or mentor in the future. Ways that he interacts with nieces and nephews, or kids on your block. Point out ways that you've seen him mentor and encourage the younger men around him. Whether you have children or not, fatherly and mentoring qualities are there and should definitely be encouraged. Start encouraging and building up that confidence now.)

Think and Journal
Make a list of ways your husband is a good dad. Circle the ones that surprise you or are different from the way you would naturally do things.

Intentional Love
Take time to look for these things and point them out in the moment.

Discussion Question
Share some of the biggest ways you feel like he has grown as a parent. Ask: What's a way you feel like you've grown as a parent?

18: GOOD DAD

THINK AND JOURNAL

INTENTIONAL LOVE

19

priority

19: PRIORITY

If you're like me, your attention can easily be diverted and divided all day long. From one need to another, I flit. I float. I fleetly flee. I fly.

And it sometimes seems, that just when I'm about to settle into really savor one of those little moments, someone yells *MOM!*

This was even true before we had kids. But instead of someone yelling *MOM!* it was a pile of papers that needed grading or my phone buzzing with a message.

We have a rule at our house that I totally stole from a friend of ours. And simply it's Blood, Destruction, or Fire. Those three things are scream-worthy, interrupt-us-no-matter-what things.

And the rest, just isn't.

This is so, so hard for me as a mom. I hear a yell, a whine, a fight breaking out. And I want to jump in, to fix, control, and "help".

But where my attention needs to be, sometimes, is right on the guy I married. He needs to know he's still my guy. The most important one in the room. He needs my eye contact and my active listening. He needs to know I'm actually present with him, not just physically there but mentally there, too.

INTENTIONAL LOVE: 31 WAYS TO LOVE YOUR *husband*

The added bonus is that our kids see that our marriage is a priority. They're learning how to interrupt politely. And we're learning what we can focus on in the present and what needs to wait until later.

For this to work, we've got to have our priorities straight. God. My husband. My kids. Everything else.

Think and Journal

Think about what tends to distract you from your husband the most often, whether that's the kids, work, phone, or something else. Then think of a few ideas for letting your husband know he's your priority and how you can show him that. Write these all down.

Intentional Love

Exercise this muscle. Now that you're more aware of what pulls you away from your husband having your attention, practice the ways that he can have more of your attention.

Discussion Question

Ask: How do you feel when you are trying to talk or be with me and I'm distracted or interrupted?

19: PRIORITY

THINK AND JOURNAL

INTENTIONAL LOVE

20

not easily angered

20: NOT EASILY ANGERED

Back when we were first married, my husband started his own business. And after months and months of saving, he bought his first smartphone.

After it arrived via FedEx, we needed to run an errand, so we jumped in the car and while he drove, I played and swiped and investigated. (And even as I write this, it sounds laughable to me just seven short years later that this sounds borderline like alien behavior.)

As I was going over his phone, I found the mini SD card which was so cute and small and new and I just had to see it and touch it. So I popped it out — just as my husband hit a bump on the road. That little, bitty, mini SD card flew into the air and then fell into the crack of no return — between the center console and my seat.

My face was completely frozen in a look of terror. I mumbled out "I'm sorry". I scooted away, to put as much distance between myself and him as I prepared for the yelling that was sure to come.

Only, it didn't.

Instead, he said, "Show me where it fell." I pointed, silent. And he said, "I'll find it when we get home."

This stands out in my head as an example of love not being easily angered. Now I have no idea what went through his head, if he was intentionally trying to love me well or what.

But I know that now, when he makes a mistake, I can stop and choose a reaction other than anger and yelling.

Sometimes that means remembering to be quiet if I can't be kind. Or it means saving a conversation until I've had time to sort out my emotions. And sometimes it means looking to see if the offense is really as bad as my initial gut reaction to it.

"Everyone should be quick to listen, slow to speak and slow to become angry" (James 1:19) is a great verse to tuck away for these instances (especially if your default has been quick, fast words and anger in the past).

Think and Journal

Do you think you're easily angered? What about your husband? What was modeled for you by your parents?

Intentional Love

Make a note card with James 1:19 on it. "My dear brothers and sisters, take note of this: Everyone should be quick to listen, slow to speak and slow to become angry" (ESV) and put the note in a place (or write it out more than once and put it in several places) you'll see it often.

Discussion Question

Take time to discuss how you and your husband would like the other person to react to a mistake. Talk about it in the moment? That evening? That weekend? The next time your husband makes a mistake, take a deep breath and try to gauge your reaction for the situation putting some of these ideas into practice.

20: NOT EASILY ANGERED

THINK AND JOURNAL

21: QUESTION GAME

On my birthday every year during college, my best friend would play the Birthday Question Game. It's not hard really nor does it take a lot of preparation. It's just a way of getting the birthday person talking, sharing, remembering, and having a little fun.

Early in my marriage, I realized that I talked a lot. Like, a lot a lot. Like, maybe my husband couldn't share his stuff because my stuff was a never-ending barrage of all the talking. Maybe. You'd have to ask him.

Anyways, as I was learning more about marriage, I kept being reminded (and reminded and reminded!) that men and women are just wired differently. While I thought I was leaving all of this time (the time it took me to inhale) for my husband to jump into a conversation, the fact is that I was making it hard for him to really share with me. He needed time and space.

So I decided that for a season, I wouldn't tell him about my day until he asked. And until he asked I'd learn as much as I could about his day, his goals, his whatever he had going on.

The first day was torture. Maybe the whole first week.

Then I channeled "The Birthday Question Game" but instead of asking him about his birthday, I would ask more specific and open-ended questions about his day, his work, all of it.

Questions like: *What was that new product you were telling me about the other day? What do you like about it? Is this a completely new thing or is it an upgrade of something else? Have you learned about the process at all? I'd love to hear about it. Do you think you'd like to get one? Tell me what you worked on today? Oh, is that part of a bigger project? And what's the goal for it? Who are you working with? Are these people you enjoy working with? Oh, what makes them challenging? You mentioned the other day that you were thinking of starting this project at home. Have you thought more about that? How can I support you in this? Is it something you were hoping to do together? Did you ever do something like this with your dad? Tell me about it. Where did you learn about this method you'll be using?*

The Birthday Question Game doesn't ask "why". Why questions are hard to answer and often put people on the defensive. The Birthday Question Game says "tell me more about this..." and then listens intently to get to know the other person better.

Think and Journal

Make a list of questions you could ask your husband to get him talking. Make these questions about him and what he's interested in.

Intentional Love

Starting today, make a habit of asking good questions to your husband. Skip the "How was your day?" and instead try "Tell me about your day. What was something hard? What was something good?"

Discussion Question

Ask: What kind of questions do you wish I'd ask more? How do you feel like you're most able to share with me?

21: QUESTION GAME

THINK AND JOURNAL

INTENTIONAL LOVE

22

career

22: CAREER

What we choose to do for a living is no small thing. For many of us, we had to get extended training or education. We work in it day in and day out. Some of us love our jobs and some of us, well, not so much.

For our husbands, where they work is often a battlefield. It's where our men of valor do their daily battle in our modern world.

Sometimes that's great. It's where they learn more things and grow and develop.

Sometimes it's not so great. It's where they are in constant competition, where they are beaten down mentally and emotionally, and made to feel small and insignificant.

My husband worked in a high-pressure corporate environment for a few years. The first year he did an entry-level job, just to get his foot in the door because he thought he really wanted to work for that company.

That first year was definitely trying, because of both his work hours and what he had to do for his job that didn't really fit his personality or skill set. The stress was heavy on his face and in how he came home every day.

Then when he moved into the job he had been hoping for, we thought everything would be so much better. And it was, but not for long. Many days he felt like a cog in the machine and that he could keep running faster and faster or get replaced.

INTENTIONAL LOVE: 31 WAYS TO LOVE YOUR *husband*

And as much as I didn't love his job, I knew he needed support from me, not more beating down.

So I thanked him for going to work. I took him lunch. I got excited about little victories so we could celebrate and focus on them.

It wasn't easy for either one of us and I'm so thankful now that he's found something that's a better fit for him. But in the years when it was our reality, it was so important to look for, see, and celebrate the good things.

No matter what your situation, try to find ways to be thankful for and encourage him in his work.

Think and Journal

Make a list of positives about your husband's job. Only the good stuff. Push yourself to get to five. That's one for each day of the work week.

Intentional Love

Start speaking the things from your list to your husband on his way out the door. One for each day as he heads to work.

Discussion Question

Ask: What are ways you feel beat down at work? How do you feel most encouraged by me?

22: CAREER

THINK AND JOURNAL

23: GO TO BED

Even if you aren't a cuddly sleeper (I totally am), there is something powerful about going to bed at the same time.

It's a small way of saying "Hey. I want to be with you." So you wrap up what you're doing, get ready for bed, and hit the sheets at the same time.

Going to bed together and just laying next to each other, reading, is easily one of my favorite parts of our day. It's slow and quiet. I can put my cold feet up against Matt's warm legs. We can rehash the craziest things our kids said or did that day. We reconnect before we fall asleep.

There are seasons where this doesn't work quite as well, like when we have a newborn or a big work deadline. After skipping going to bed at the same time in those seasons, we've found ways to work around it.

We've laid down together for just a few minutes until the baby monitor goes off and lets us know someone needs us.

One of us has gotten back up to finish a work project.

Someone on the LATCC Facebook page who works different shifts than her husband said they go to bed twice a day, just to spend that brief time together before one falls asleep.

Our beds offer literal and figurative comfort, a soft and safe place to land.

INTENTIONAL LOVE: 31 WAYS TO LOVE YOUR *husband*

Going to bed at the same time extends a hand of invitation to both of us to jump into the comfort our bed offers and let it wash over us, to let the soft place to land extend between the two of us, and to reconnect in the middle of that.

Think and Journal

What prevents you from being able to go to bed at the same time? Make a list.

Intentional Love

Set an alarm to remind yourselves to stop what you're doing for the day and head to bed. Invite your husband to come with you. Read, talk, pray, and wind down together before sleeping.

Discussion Question

Ask: What do you like about going to bed at the same time? What do you find challenging about it?

23: GO TO BED

THINK AND JOURNAL

24: PHYSICAL ATTRACTIVENESS

I went to a marriage conference years ago where the pastor shared that on the day he got married, he started praying that his wife would be his standard for beauty for his whole life. And I was so struck by the simplicity of this, that I repeated it to my husband several times as something I thought was really cool.

And only in the last few years have I realized that it works both ways, really.

What if our husbands were our standard for physical attractiveness?

What if, instead of Man Crush Monday's on Instagram and The Eye Candy board on Pinterest of celebrities, we dedicated our #mcm to our husbands?

What if we didn't see movies like *Magic Mike* or read books like *50 Shades* or even romance novels, so that we wouldn't create a completely fake scenario in our head that our husbands can never hope to measure up to?

What if we prayed and asked God to make our husbands, the way he is, our standard of physical attractiveness? That we would find him sexy, desirable, and attractive?

All of these things, the Man Crush Mondays, Celebrity Eye Candy boards, and the erotica parading as "romantic love stories", create lands, thoughts, and situations of pure fantasy. And our living, breathing, flesh, and blood husbands can't measure up to a perfectly curated and airbrushed scenario that we carry around in our heads.

INTENTIONAL LOVE: 31 WAYS TO LOVE YOUR *husband*

I know I for one would not want to be competing with an image my husband was carrying around in his head.

And he doesn't want to have to compete with one, either.

Think and Journal

Write a prayer asking God to make your husband your standard of physical attractiveness. If this is something that seems super strange to you because it's not something you've ever prayed about before, make a list of things you find attractive about your husband physically. And ask God to help increase your awareness of these things.

Intentional Love

When you're talking to your husband over the next few days, try touching the parts of his body that you find attractive.

Discussion Question

Share the areas of the body that you find the most attractive about each other. Remember these are specific physical attributes.

24: PHYSICAL ATTRACTIVENESS

THINK AND JOURNAL

INTENTIONAL LOVE

25

sex

25: SEX

"I know I'm supposed to be having sex with my husband. GAH!" That's often the reaction by women when someone brings up sex in a marriage talk or book. It's ok. Get it out of your system.

For some of us, growing up during hardcore purity culture, sex feels "bad" somehow. We had no idea how to flip the "switch" when we got married and still really aren't sure how. We want to be present and active in our sex life but what does that look like?

Some of us have baggage from past mistakes. We can't seem to shake the thoughts that come up when we want to be all in with our husbands.

For others of us, we're tired, tapped, and touched out. We want to sleep for a few years and try again when we've gotten some sleep.

And I think all of us know how important sex is for our marriages. We want to work at it. And we would love to enjoy it.

Know that sex is more than physical. Yes, it's obvious physical oneness, a great image for what's happening emotionally and spiritually.

Emotionally, specific hormones like oxytocin, dopamine, and vasopressin are released and these hormones actually build the emotional bond in your marriage by making you feel closer, making you want to be faithful to that one person, and making you want to do it again and again — increasing the emotional bond each time.

INTENTIONAL LOVE: 31 WAYS TO LOVE YOUR *husband*

It's also spiritual. God created it as a way to bind us to our husbands in every way.

Married sex, the way God created it and intended it to be, isn't dirty. It isn't a duty. It's a delight. A gift for just you and your husband to build your relationship in a really unique and special way.

Think and Journal

How do you feel about your sex life? How do you wish it could grow? Write down some honest thoughts.

Intentional Love

Create a "toolkit" to help you transition from your day-to-day-ness to Smokin' Hot Mama. Include items like perfume, deodorant, lip gloss, mouthwash, something you feel sexy in — basically items that will help you shake off the grumps or frumps and refresh.

Discussion Question

Talk about ways you can help each other make sex a priority.

25: SEX

THINK AND JOURNAL

INTENTIONAL LOVE

26

sleep

26: SLEEP

Sleep is getting its own category outside of self-care because it's super important.

I know for a lot of years I thought I could burn the candle at both ends. I could work late, grading papers, watching Friends, and get up early to make breakfast and have quiet time before work.

Now I'm not even sure I can burn the candle at one end.

Some nights, I want to go to bed as I put supper on the table. And getting up early in the morning? Forget about it.

There is a certain allure to the midnight hour when the house is quiet, and (maybe) picked up-ish, and you can have some deep breath time, some read a book time, some watch the show you want to watch time.

But to have anything to give to the other people in your house, you have got to have something in your own tank.

And a great place to start is with sleep.

Sleep often seems to be the first thing we're willing to sacrifice to create more time in our day.

As much as I LOVE coffee, I know that a woman does not live by coffee alone. We need rest. God created us for rest. He even gave us a whole day for it.

INTENTIONAL LOVE: 31 WAYS TO LOVE YOUR *husband*

Think and Journal

How many hours of sleep would be ideal? Work backward from your required wake-up time and figure out when you need to be going to bed. What's getting in the way of that? What habits can you change to make getting to bed easier? Make a list of ideas and even create an ideal nightly routine, including when devices get turned off, when you need to be in bed, and when you need to go to sleep.

Intentional Love

Go to bed when you need to tonight. Extend an invitation for your husband to come with you so he can get the sleep he needs too.

Discussion Question

Make a plan for more sleep. Talk through your bedtime routines and find ways to support each other. Maybe it means getting a sleep mask for one of you so the other can read longer. Maybe it means getting different sheets that are more comfortable or room darkening curtains to block light. Take some time to talk through it.

26: SLEEP

THINK AND JOURNAL

27: DO SOMETHING TOGETHER

At our house, I am lovingly referred to as the "evangelist" while my husband calls himself the "researcher". He reads and learns all of these things, has all of the blogs and podcasts that he follows and tells me about. I nod along and smile, but until I experience something, I never get why it's so exciting. Then once I experience it, I can't shut up about it; I have to share it with everyone.

I can't remember exactly when my husband mentioned stand up paddleboarding but I do know that for several weeks, many of his stories would start with "so I was reading this thing on stand up paddleboarding…." and I would try to picture it in my head or follow along or any number of things, but mostly I didn't get it.

So after he had talked about it for about a year I thought "well I'll buy him one of those stander upper things and he'll love it" only they are a little out of our budget so I started thinking about other options.

We live in a lake town, and I saw here that you can rent them. *Perfect* I thought to myself. *I'll send him out for a day of paddleboarding.*

But as we talked about the idea of me giving him an activity to go and do by himself, he asked me if I wanted to come.

Spending time together for us is very different. I've learned that for him, he just likes me being there, sharing the experience, in what I call shoulder-to-shoulder time. And for me, I want our time together to be interactive and connecting, which I call face-to-face time.

INTENTIONAL LOVE: 31 WAYS TO LOVE YOUR *husband*

So I knew that what he was inviting me to do was to share an experience with him. Understand why he was so interested, not talk about all the things. But to be able to do more than ask questions like "So it's a surfboard but no one is surfing?" and say "Ok, tell me again how people use this thing."

Part of what made it so great was learning something new together. It could have been anything, like rolling sushi, or cardio kickboxing, but just taking the first step together was super cool and connecting.

But then to do it, learn it, and have the memories to talk about it together just really makes it so awesome — and so simple — to do something together.

Think and Journal

What is something you have done with your husband in the past? What are some of your favorite memories from that event? What is something you would really like to do or learn with your husband?

Intentional Love

Do something together tonight. Take a walk. Make a meal. Do the dishes. Focus on the being together. And savoring that time.

Discussion Question

Ask: What is something you'd really love to do or learn to do? How do you see us doing that together or is it something you'd like to do as part of self-care?

27: DO SOMETHING TOGETHER

THINK AND JOURNAL

28: YES & NO

Often when we consider a commitment, a new thing to add to our lives, we focus on the calendar and how full it is, and we check the bank account, but forget that each yes means fuller and fuller lives which have an impact on our mental and emotional capacities, too.

When I have reached top capacity, I notice that it impacts me emotionally first.

And my emotional capacity (or serious lack thereof) starts leaking into all the other aspects of my life.

Over this month, as you're looking at adding date nights or intentional time to spend with your husband, think about things that are in your life that could go. Physical stuff, that will leave you with less to clean and maintain. Maybe some line items from your budget that make it feel tight. Calendar commitments that leave you feeling drained and running on E without being filled up. And definitely things that deplete your emotional capacity.

Our best yes's comes from considering not just the calendar slots and the dollars and cents column but also how we will feel emotionally and mentally.

For me, right now, especially in seasons of pretty serious sleep deprivation with babies, I haven't got a lot to give emotionally. So my calendar can't be so full that I have no rest and recuperation time.

However, dates and date nights are really emotionally life-giving. So then I'll gladly hand out no's to all the other things so I can get a date with my husband. I'll even lose a little sleep. That's how much it fills me up.

INTENTIONAL LOVE: 31 WAYS TO LOVE YOUR *husband*

So as you're looking at what you're trying to add into this month, know that I'm not saying to add more hours to your day since none of us can do that. What I am saying is to create time and space by looking at what can go and realizing that our best yes's come from a lot of no's and has a lot more to it than our calendar.

Think and Journal

Is there anything about a normal week for you that makes you feel depleted, over capacity, completely tapped? Sometimes the thing that we think is the culprit of feeling tapped (like having little kids for example) is really just a reminder of where our best yes lies and shows us that we need to back off in other areas. Start thinking about and praying about things that are life giving to you and things that are not. Make a list of them to help you see what can get added in and what can go.

Intentional Love

Toys are the never-ending cleanup story at my house. And when they left me frazzled and fried, I made a new system for clean up that has made the end of the day much less stressful. What's an emotional-capacity saving thing you could try today? Maybe it's a toy system. Maybe it's using paper plates. Maybe it's not signing up for baseball. Maybe it's letting the kids go a couple more days in between baths. Think of something to save your emotional capacity.

Discussion Question

Ask: What are some things that completely drain us? What are things that are really life-giving to us? Is there a way we can work to minimize the things that drain us?

28: YES & NO

THINK AND JOURNAL

29: LITTLE MOMENTS

It is not often in our current life stage that my husband and I can have an hours-long conversation without being interrupted. Sometimes it's not even a minutes-long conversation before someone needs us.

And that's ok. It's the reality of the season we're in with four little people.

I would love it if we could sit and talk for hours. But there will come a day again when this house will be silent except for our typing fingers and our phones buzzing nonstop with our children and grandchildren calling or texting us daily. (Hey, a girl can dream...)

Until then, I'm not going to sit and wait for "picture perfect" to drop in my lap. I'm going to savor the little moments we do get together.

Recently we were returning home from a trip to visit our families. We settled all of the kids in the van with toys and books and then we started a conversation. Maybe 10 minutes. We stopped and looked around. It was still quiet.

So we started another one.

Then another one.

We got interrupted a few times but we chose to continue to savor the moments we did have. To talk and make the most of them. To hold hands. To dream. To share new ideas and pieces of ourselves.

INTENTIONAL LOVE: 31 WAYS TO LOVE YOUR *husband*

Marriage isn't the big stuff, even though that tends to be what we remember.

Marriage is the little stuff, the day to day, minute to minute choosing each other and making each other a priority.

So savor the moments you get together. Not every date night/day/breakfast/movie/minute will be magical fireworks and unicorns. Sometimes it will be normal. Ordinary. Interrupted. That doesn't make it less beautiful. Have fun. Laugh. Smile. Touch. Flirt.

Think and Journal

Where are you most likely to get little moments in your day? Where can you create little moments? Like we send the kids to play while we clean up dinner, giving us time to connect and talk mostly uninterrupted. Are there times like that in your day? Write them down.

Intentional Love

Create a moment today of three uninterrupted minutes. You can find ideas for how to do this in the resource section at the back of the book.

Discussion Questions

Talk about your favorite little moments of the day or week. Talk about ways you can create more of them.

29: LITTLE MOMENTS

THINK AND JOURNAL

30: HAVE FUN

When was the last time you had fun with your husband? I mean something light, something that made you laugh, something honest to goodness just fun?

I think this is one of those things that can, like kissing, just seem to fade away.

Life gets harder, more serious, and has more things to discuss so that fun seems harder. It seems harder to just let loose for a night. To really just belly laugh.

And maybe, too, it feels a little irresponsible when you know you have all of this serious life stuff, and grown up stuff, so checking out for a day or a night or even an hour feels like not the most grown up choice.

When I was in labor with our 2nd baby, my water broke, but then nothing happened. We waited for hours in the hospital, hoping labor would start on its own. And there's nothing quite so stressful as waiting in a hospital.

So we thought we'd lighten it up by watching some Jim Gaffigan comedy specials.

Every time a nurse would walk in the room, we'd get a weird look. But instead of letting the stress of waiting take over, we decided to have a little fun.

INTENTIONAL LOVE: 31 WAYS TO LOVE YOUR *husband*

That saying "laughter is the best medicine" didn't happen by accident. People laughing and really enjoying themselves tends to make them feel tons better.

It's ok to take a day, a night, or an hour, to have fun, laugh at yourself and your husband, and come back, refreshed and ready for all the grown up stuff.

Think and Journal

What is something that you really like to do for fun? Or something that really makes you laugh? Maybe it's learning something new that you know you'll be bad at. Or watching a comedy special. Or going on a spontaneous road trip. Write down your ideas.

Intentional Love

Plan to do something together, just fun, just for the two of you. If you can, find something fun to do tonight even, like play a game, watch a comedy, or anything that will have you laughing.

Discussion Question

Ask: What is one of your funniest memories ever? What is one of your funniest memories from our wedding or marriage?

30: HAVE FUN

THINK AND JOURNAL

INTENTIONAL LOVE

31

go out

31: GO OUT

Ok, you've carved out time and worked on a ton of habits that show intentional love in the every-day-ness.

A lot of this might have kicked up memories of when you first started dating and looking around now, I'm guessing your life is not at all like when you first started dating — and probably in some pretty amazing ways.

Tonight, it's time to celebrate. Time to sit somewhere, just you and your husband, and talk about the amazing, subtle, obvious, big, and small changes you've seen over the last month.

So put on something you look and feel great in. Freshen up in your preferred way and head out! (Aren't you glad now you listened to me about that babysitter thing for tonight!?)

You did it! You spent a month being intentional in your marriage, carving out time and attention, in the middle of whatever else you had going on, to make your marriage a priority.

But what you've done here doesn't end tonight. This is just the start of taking notice, making a priority, in a new way.

I am so honored to have walked this with you. And so proud of the heart work you've done this month.

You go, girl.

Now, get outta here. Grab your books if you need to for talking about the last month. Go enjoy your date night!

INTENTIONAL LOVE: 31 WAYS TO LOVE YOUR *husband*

Think and Journal

Which day was your favorite? Which habit have you enjoyed working on the most? Which has been the most challenging?

Intentional Love

Go on a date. If you couldn't get a sitter tonight, do it after the kids are in bed or go out in a couple of days. But don't wait too long!

Discussion Question

Discuss the last month together. Bring your books and share your favorite and hardest days. Let this be a memorial stone to the last month you spent working on being intentional in your marriage.

(And take a picture for Facebook or Instagram and use the hashtag *#intentionallove31*. We can't wait to share the excitement with you!)

31: GO OUT

THINK AND JOURNAL

INTENTIONAL LOVE

32+

perseveres

32⁺: PERSEVERES

Wow. We really are so thankful and honored that you would walk through 31 days of your marriage with us, using simple, intentional acts of love to spark a fire in your marriage.

We know this past month hasn't been easy. You've worked on all kinds of habits, had hard discussions, looked at schedules, and even learned and relearned some things.

In some ways, you're probably exhausted and glad to see the back side of this book.

And in other ways, you're probably exhilarated, set ablaze with thoughts and ideas that will drive you forward to continue these new habits of intentionality in your marriage.

(Don't worry, you can be both.)

Remember that what you've started here and the work you've begun doesn't end today.

You might circle back around to specific topics as you need them. You might find yourself focusing on three or four that were really impactful. And you might find yourself flipping through these pages again one day, in another season, in another time, to remember and relearn these building blocks.

Marriage is a marathon. Love perseveres. And the things that impact our marriage the most are the small moments that fill up our lives.

INTENTIONAL LOVE: 31 WAYS TO LOVE YOUR husband

I want to leave you with one final thought on love persevering.

When I was 23 years old, I got up in front of a church, and said some beautiful vows that I planned on living out for the rest of my life, until I was 103 and we could be married 80 years, if the Lord willed it.

Only, what I didn't know about marriage *exactly* when I got married (there are lots of things we KNOW but until we live and experience them we don't <u>really</u> KNOW) was that I was signing up to run a marathon as a three-legged race with a guy who would change and grow and be different over all the different stages of our life, and he would be living with and loving a girl who was not at all like the girl who stood up in front of the church that day.

Now imagine yourselves as a couple who have been married for 60 years standing up in front of the family you've cultivated and cared for as you renew your wedding vows. The words "til death us do part" offer a different perspective when you're closer to it than you were the first time you said those same words.

Marriage is all about perseverance; continuing through each difficulty and challenge and looking at it as a journey, a marathon.

And we sign up to do it together becoming one, while also still very much wanting what we want and learning how to meld those together, like a three-legged race.

32⁺: PERSEVERES

But there is no one on this earth I'd rather three-legged race with than my husband.

Because I know, when life is at its hardest — and we've known some hard seasons — that he's not leaving the race. He's not dragging me along as collateral damage. His arm is wrapped around me as we support one another through it.

And when life isn't quite at it's hardest, we can work together to increase the pace or decrease it for a little bit of respite.

We hope and pray that these small, intentional moments you've learned and grown would be life-giving in your marriage. That you would choose to assume goodwill from your spouse, even when they don't totally get it right. That you would remember that what you look for is what you see. That you would extend grace to your spouse and to yourself as you grow in these ways throughout your whole marriage and life together.

Intentional Love doesn't end today. *Intentional Love* is the actions and thoughtfulness and purpose that you put into moving forward from today.

One last thing before you go, we want you to know that God loves you. He knew you before He made the world and He intentionally and thoughtfully stitched you together for a reason and a purpose. You are deeply loved by your Creator. And yes, this book is about marriage, but the love of your marriage is meant to be a taste of the love God has for you.

INTENTIONAL LOVE: 31 WAYS TO LOVE YOUR *husband*

Thank you for doing this past month with us. It has been our joy to walk through this with you. We'd love to stay in touch and find out what you learned during your time in *Intentional Love*. Use hashtag *#intentionallove31* or see our contact page in the back of the book.

We wish you many happy years of love in your marriage.

— Matt and Leah

32⁺: PERSEVERES

THINK AND JOURNAL

INTENTIONAL LOVE
discussion questions

DISCUSSION QUESTIONS

What can I be praying for you over the course of the next week?

1: Talk about what you'd like your love story legacy to be and how you want to share that with your kids.

2: Ask: What types of things do you wish I'd notice more? When do you feel the most seen: When you are thanked/acknowledged? When you are given a break from those things? When you are helped with those things? When you're given affirmations for those things?

3: Ask: How do you like to be thanked? With a note, gesture, in the moment, later, in front of people, or privately? Talk about your preferences.

4: Ask: In what ways do you feel like I'm most/least patient with you?

5: We all know there are challenging things we will still see in our marriages and in each other. Ask: How would you like me to approach topics when change might be required?

6: Ask: What is something you do every day that makes you think of me? Share one of your own.

7: Ask: Why do you think you are the kind of sorry-sayer you are? Was it modeled for you? Did you have to become a peacemaker in some way? Did you not see people apologize?

INTENTIONAL LOVE: 31 WAYS TO LOVE YOUR *husband*

8: Discuss your ideal intentional time at home. Is there a meal? A theme? A pattern? Different all the time?

9: Ask: How do you feel when you overhear me talking negatively about you in a group? How do you feel when you overhear me talking positively about you in a group?

10: Ask: How do you feel normally in a conversation about your dreams? How would you like me to respond?

11: Ask: When does my tech time bother you the most? Listen to each other's ideas and work to not let technology continue to be a distraction for your marriage.

12: Ask: If there is an issue I would like to talk with you about, how can I handle it in a way that makes you feel loved and cared for?

13: Ask: What are some of your favorite ways to connect through touch? How can we increase these occurrences?

14: Ask: What's a way I swoop in, nag, badger, or steamroll you in something you say you'll take care of? How can I support you better?

15: Sit down and talk about carving time out for both of you to get some self-care time. Maybe that's trading a couple hours every other Saturday. Maybe it's after the kids are in bed one night a week. Maybe it's on your lunch hour from work. Put it on the calendar.

DISCUSSION QUESTIONS

16: Share how you give and receive love, especially if they're different. Ask: What are five ways I could make you feel the most loved?

17: Ask: What is something specific you enjoy when I kiss you?

18: Share some of the biggest ways you feel like he has grown as a parent. Ask: What's a way you feel like you've grown as a parent?

19: Ask: How do you feel when you are trying to talk or be with me and I'm distracted or interrupted?

20: Take time to discuss how you would like the other person to react to a mistake. Talk about it in the moment? That evening? That weekend? The next time your spouse makes a mistake, take a deep breath and try to gauge your reaction for the situation putting some of these ideas into practice.

21: Ask: What kind of questions do you wish I'd ask more? How do you feel like you're most able to share with me?

22: Ask: What are ways you feel beat down at work? How do you feel most encouraged by me?

23: Ask: What do you like about going to bed at the same time? What do you find challenging about it?

24: Share the areas of the body that you find the most attractive about each other. Remember these are physical qualities.

INTENTIONAL LOVE: 31 WAYS TO LOVE YOUR *husband*

25: Talk about ways you can help each other make sex a priority, like scheduling it, having some regroup time after the kids go to bed.

26: Make a plan for more sleep. Talk through your bedtime routines and find ways to support each other. Maybe it means getting a sleep mask for one of you so the other can read longer. Maybe it means getting different sheets that are more comfortable or room darkening curtains to block light. Take some time to talk through it.

27: Ask: What is something you'd really love to do or learn to do? How do you see us doing that together or is it something you'd like to do as part of self-care?

28: Ask: What are some things that completely drain us? What are things that are really life-giving to us? Is there a way we can work to minimize the things that drain us? What do you think?

29: Talk about your favorite little moments of the day or week. Talk about ways you can create more of them.

30: Ask: What is one of your funniest memories ever? What is one of your funniest memories from our wedding or marriage?

31: Discuss the last month together. Bring your books and share your favorite and hardest days. Let this be a memorial stone to the last month you spent working on being intentional in your marriage.

RESOURCE PAGE

You can find printable discussion questions, blog posts, books, and other information that will help you grow in your journey of Intentional Love on the resource page for this book.

leahheffner.com/intentional-love-resources

FIND US ONLINE

Matt and Leah are working to cultivate, by God's grace, a life of intentionality in their marriage, parenting, and work. They write, speak, and encourage online, while being learn-as-they-go homesteaders, travelers, and homeschooling their ever-growing gaggle of kids. You can find their encouraging line of lifestyle products at *TheRedOakCollective.com*

We'd love to chat with you online. Head to one of these spots to give us a shout!

Websites
leahheffner.com

ourdailyrest.net

theredoakcollective.com

Facebook
facebook.com/LifeAroundTheCoffeeCup

facebook.com/thedailyrest

Instagram
instagram.com/leahheffner

instagram.com/ourdailyrest

#intentionallove31

ABOUT LEAH HEFFNER

Leah is the wife to a sexy, beard-sporting, man of God and mom to four cutie-pie-heads. She's a new southerner, a sometimes-DIYer, and a novice gardener. She loves coffee, a good Netflix binge, and encouraging other women.

She wants you to know that she's totally just a normal mom. A normal wife. The majority of her day is taken up by wiping butts, playing farm animals, ignoring dried sweet potatoes on the floor, running errands, and pretending she has a plan for dinner (shh don't tell, ok?).

But she loves being real and over-eager as she shares about marriage and motherhood as we grow by God's grace.

You can find Leah online at *leahheffner.com* where she offers encouragement in marriage, motherhood, faith, and friendship.

You can find her on:
Facebook: *facebook.com/LifeAroundTheCoffeeCup*
and Instagram: *instagram.com/LeahHeffner*

ABOUT MATT HEFFNER

After being diagnosed with Crohn's Disease a decade ago, Matt's been on a journey to live a life that cultivates restfulness and balance among all the things that God has given him. He loves being outside, having a good laugh with his wife, and giving "piggy back" rides to his tireless kids. He's also the founder of Our Daily Rest.

He's a learn-as-he-goes homesteader with a flock of chickens, traveler, and business owner whose joy it is to share and encourage others in their journey of intentionality in the different parts of their lives.

You can find Matt online at *ourdailyrest.net* where he hosts a blog and podcast to help you cultivate a lifestyle of restfulness, balance, wellness, and renewal in all aspects of your life.

You can find him on:
Facebook: *facebook.com/thedailyrest*
and Instagram: *instagram.com/ourdailyrest*

DO MORE. HAVE MORE. BE MORE.

Those are the messages we are bombarded with all day long from all around us.

But that's not what our soul needs.

What our soul needs is encouragement, gentle reminders, and truth.

And wouldn't it be nice if it came in great designs, with quality sayings and quotes, and stuff that you'd actually want to wear or have hanging in your house?

It is our passion to encourage other people. And with The Red Oak Collective, it is our hope to encourage others with the products they have in their homes. We've carefully designed and curated quality lifestyle products you'll enjoy for years to come.

Encouragement for your soul, full of truth.

Check out The Red Oak Collective: *theredoakcollective.com*

DO MORE. HAVE MORE. BE MORE.

Those are the messages we are bombarded with all day long from all around us.

But that's not what our soul needs.

What our soul needs is encouragement, gentle reminders, and truth.

And wouldn't it be nice if it came in great designs, with quality sayings and quotes, and stuff that you'd actually want to wear or have hanging in your house?

It is our passion to encourage other people. And with The Red Oak Collective, it is our hope to encourage others with the products they have in their homes. We've carefully designed and curated quality lifestyle products you'll enjoy for years to come.

Encouragement for your soul, full of truth.

Check out The Red Oak Collective: *theredoakcollective.com*

www.ingramcontent.com/pod-product-compliance
Lightning Source LLC
Chambersburg PA
CBHW071500070426
42452CB00041B/1948

Vivian Elebiyo-Okojie

ELEVIV PUBLISHING GROUP
HOUSTON, TEXAS

SAY YES TO LIFE

Copyright © 2015 by Vivian Okojie

All rights reserved. No part of this book may be reproduced or transmitted in any form or by any means without written permission of the author.

ISBN: 978-0692427231